In Him Was Life

Four Dramas
For Lent And Easter

Karren Boehr

CSS Publishing Company, Inc., Lima, Ohio

IN HIM WAS LIFE

Copyright © 1997 by
CSS Publishing Company, Inc.
Lima, Ohio

All rights reserved. No part of this publication may be reproduced in any manner whatsoever without the prior permission of the publisher, except in the case of brief quotations embodied in critical articles and reviews. Inquiries should be addressed to: Permissions, CSS Publishing Company, Inc., P.O. Box 4503, Lima, Ohio 45802-4503.

Scripture quotations are taken from the *New American Standard Bible*, © 1960, 1962, 1963, 1968, 1971, 1972, 1073, 1975, 1977 by The Lockman Foundation. Used by permission.

ISBN 0-7880-1130-8　　　　　　　　　　　　　　　PRINTED IN U.S.A.

To Stan:
who puts up with
my theatrics
on a daily basis

Table Of Contents

1. The Lenten Car Pool   7
2. In Him Was Life   13
3. Judas   17
4. He Is Risen   21

THE LENTEN CAR POOL

A Modern Drama For Lent

The message of this play is laid out in a format that even the newest of Christians can easily understand and apply — that Christ is risen and alive in the hearts of men.

Setting: Inside of a dilapidated car

Props: Two stools, two dinner buckets, morning newspaper, banana

Characters:
CHARLIE: A nice enough guy, crude, easygoing, not excited about spiritual things
BOB: Tough-looking man, quiet-mannered, genuine

Costumes: Both men are dressed in work clothes, caps

(Bob is sitting on the right stool as if he were driving a car. His dinner bucket is on the floor beside him. He fidgets, looks around, adjusts the mirrors, finally opens newspaper.)

CHARLIE: *(Running in from left, slides onto the other stool. Panting)* Sorry ... I'm late ... The alarm didn't go off this morning, and then I couldn't find my work shoes — had to wear my Nikes, and the boss will probably have a fit. But then what else is new? Dog must have buried those suckers good.

BOB: *(Puts down newspaper and starts driving. For a while he doesn't respond)* Whew, looks like everyone overslept this morning. Would you look at all this traffic!

CHARLIE: *(Yawning)* Did you watch the fight last night?

BOB: Fight? The wife and I took the kids to the park, and they were so dirty we ended up giving them all a shower. Then I had to gas up this crate. After that I was bushed. Turned in early.

CHARLIE: Hey, man, you used to never miss boxing on TV! You loved all that blood and guts. I mean, last night, there was red spurting all over the place ...

BOB: *(Interrupting)* Charlie, got any idea what you're going to give up for Lent?

CHARLIE: *(Surprised)* Huh? Whatcha talking about?

BOB: Lent. You know, the forty days before Easter that Christians use to remember what Christ did for them on the cross.

CHARLIE: *(Totally disinterested)* Oh, that. Naw, I'm not into that religion stuff. *(Opens lunch pail and surveys contents)* I knew it. I just knew it! I saw that moldy piece of lunchmeat in the refrigerator last night, and guess what. It's in my sandwich. My wife's nursing a burr for me — again. Women, I'll never understand them!

BOB: I'm giving up TV.

CHARLIE: You're giving up TV for Lent? Bobby, my boy, you are one nuts guy. If you've got to give up something, why not make it ... ah ... lipstick. Or radishes. If you really want to go all out, why not try ... toothpaste. But TV?

BOB: Yep. TV is the thing I would probably miss the most. Think of all the time I can spend in prayer and Bible reading that would otherwise be taken up by television yuck.

CHARLIE: Well, tell you what, you're going to miss some pretty big fights coming up. Whoa, and the NBA finals ... Man, you are one nuts guy.

BOB: I reckon you're right. You could say that — nuts about a man who died for me 2,000 years ago on a cross. He arose from the dead, too, you know. The only man to do that.

CHARLIE: *(Takes a banana from lunch box and takes a bite)* Didn't have time for breakfast. *(Pause)* You really believe that stuff? Dying on a cross and rising from the dead? Watch out! That truck ... whew! *(Looking behind him)* That was close!

BOB: *(Checking in rearview mirror)* Looks like that guy started drinking a bit early this morning. Must have a lot of troubles to drown. Life's great! Too bad he doesn't know about a Savior who loves him.

CHARLIE: Hey, what's with all this religious stuff this morning? *(Reaches for the newspaper on Bob's lap and opens it)*

BOB: Guess Christ has made such a difference in my life, I just want everyone to have the same thing. I used to worry, I used to swear, I used to fight, I hated everything and everybody, even my kids and my wife. I was one tough dude. Why, even you were afraid to associate with me.

CHARLIE: Hey, man, your temper was awful. I saw you give a foot to your dog many a time. It wasn't a pretty sight, either. I'm no dumb rock. I stayed out of your way!

BOB: *(Sighs)* You're right. But that's behind me now. It's the cross, Charlie, it's the cross. The cross of Jesus Christ has set me free. Man, I feel wonderful.

CHARLIE: You don't swear anymore, that much I'll give you ... and come to think about it, your temper's all but gone. Whew, yesterday, when that new guy ran into you with that forklift 'cause he was goofing around, I though you'd go straight into the trees. But you didn't.

BOB: Nope, Charlie. Jesus paid the price for my temper. I'm a new creature, man. Brand-new. No more temper for this guy.

CHARLIE: Come on! You're telling me if your wife packed you a moldy piece of meat in your lunch like I've got today that you wouldn't clean a few plows?

BOB: Nope. Maybe she's sore for a reason. Maybe she's not sore at all. Maybe she didn't even know the meat was moldy. It's the cross, Charlie, it's the cross.

CHARLIE: You always keep coming back to this "cross" thing! I don't get it.

BOB: It's not hard at all. Jesus was the Son of God. When He died for you and me, He paid the price for all of our sins. You and I are free, pal. All we have to do is accept His gift of saving us. Ask Him to take over our lives. It's as simple as that. Then watch the fireworks fly! Well, here we are. *(Looks at watch)* Hey, we're even four minutes early. I can't believe it. *(Hands Charlie his lunch pail)* Here, car pool buddy, let's swap today.

CHARLIE: *(Objects)* You're kidding! There's a moldy sandwich in there. And, I've already made off with the banana.

BOB: So? Let's just say I've never eaten a moldy sandwich. It might be a new experience. *(Takes Charlie's lunch pail and crawls out of car)*

CHARLIE: *(Crawling out of car)* Ah ... Bob ... this Lent thing. Think I could give up something? You know ... seeing as how this Jesus thing is sort of new to me. Man, I've seen what it's done for you, and it can't be all bad. Maybe I'll give up the fights! Yes, I'll give up the fights.

BOB: *(Gives Charlie a high five)* Look, guy, the cross of Jesus is working on you already.

CHARLIE: *(Laughs)* Hey, you may be right. See you tonight.

BOB: You got it!

(Each walks off in different direction)

IN HIM WAS LIFE

A Biblical Character Play

This play requires little space and can easily be produced among any backdrops or decor a sanctuary normally utilizes for Easter Sunday. The depth of this drama lies in the character of Peter, who is free to share his deep feelings with the audience.

Setting: A secluded place outside Jerusalem

Props: Two low rugged boxes or stumps suitable for sitting

Characters:
PETER: The Disciple of Jesus
SIMON: Peter's friend, also a follower of Jesus
1ST WOMAN
2ND WOMAN

Time: Resurrection morning

Costumes: Biblical dress

(Peter and Simon enter from right. Simon moves to a box left. He collapses in front of it, using it to lean upon. Peter, in turn, paces as the two discuss the events since the crucifixion. They remain in hiding as they sort out their innermost feelings.)

PETER: *(Sits down on a box, head in hands. It is obvious that he is in distress)* Simon, who would have thought my life would end like this? *(Pause)* Me ... the practical, levelheaded one.

SIMON: *(Shakes head and looks downcast at the floor)* Peter ... I don't know what to say.

PETER: *(Looks up, rambles slowly to himself)* Oh, life was good. I certainly wasn't looking for anything different. All I had was an ordinary fishing fleet, but it was more than enough. How I loved the sea ... the call of the gulls, the spray against my face, mending the nets along the shore.

And then He came along ... the one they called Christ. Oh, I remember it all so well. There He stood against the shoreline. *(Pause)* There was a strength in His eyes like I had never seen before. His countenance completely unearthed me. Suddenly, in the shadow of His presence, my fishing seemed to be so meaningless. I didn't know who He was; all He said was, "Follow Me." *(Whispering)* "Follow Me and I will make you fishers of men."

Yes, the words were very strange, but, Simon, my actions were far stranger. I — with a growing family to feed — knew what I needed to do. It was that clear. I laid down my nets ... and, well, you know the rest.

(Rises and walks to center stage) I, Peter, a sensible, logical man, gave up a lucrative fishing business to wander the hills of Galilee and Judea, never knowing where I would sleep, what I would eat, or even when I would see my family again. *(Goes to Simon, kneels, and shakes his shoulders to make him understand)* It's mad! What kind of father would forsake his family at a time when they needed him most!

(Still kneeling, gazes into space) And I was happy. Yes, I was truly happy ... fulfilled ... so ALIVE. Being with this man called Christ was an experience I can't put into words ... but if you could see my heart, you would understand. *(Quietly)* To experience His looks of compassion as the day drew long and His energy was far beyond being spent ... how He healed the sick ... how He gently touched the children ... the hours He spent in prayer ... the days He sat patiently teaching the twelve of us.

(Standing) I often asked myself, "Peter, do you realize how ridiculous this appears to the world? A grown man tagging behind a vagabond teacher with no place to lay His head. A teacher who

claims He is the Christ, the long-awaited One, the one whom the leaders of the church claim is strictly a phony? *(Pause)* But I couldn't leave His side. It was as if rivers of living water flowed over every molecule of my being whenever I was with Him. I hung on to His every word. Simon, this might sound strange to you, but I was never physically hungry in His presence. I never became tired. His words, His nearness, were everything to me. I needed nothing else.

And then they came and took Him away. They took away my Lord, and my world caved in around me. No, it couldn't be so! I had not asked to become a disciple. I would have been, forever, happy with my boat and fish. "So, Peter, you made a mistake," you say, "but it's not too late. Go back to your fish. The boat is still there."

(Kneels again before Simon) Ah, my friend, but you don't understand. I have felt His presence. I have seen His eyes. His message still burns within me. The rest of the world is so dim, so empty and void when compared to His marvelous face.

(Two women enter from left, excitedly. They are running and shouting.)

1ST WOMAN: Peter! Simon! We saw an angel in shining white who told us the Christ is risen! He is risen!

SIMON: Risen?

2ND WOMAN: Yes, Simon, yes! Just as He said! On our way here we met Mary. She has seen Him.

1ST WOMAN: The angel said to come and tell Peter ...

PETER: *(Interrupts)* Mary has seen Him ... the angel said to come and tell Peter?

2ND WOMAN: *(Still excited)* Yes, Peter, He is risen just as He said.

PETER: But I went to the tomb this morning. It was empty ... I thought someone had stolen his body ... *(jumps to feet)* It was empty! *(Shakes Simon by the shoulders)* Simon, the tomb was empty! My Savior lives! Jesus Christ, my Lord and Master, has risen from the grave! The knowing is suddenly within me, so full, so powerful I feel my very soul bursting with thanksgiving and praise. My Savior is alive! I am alive! Simon, it is no longer I who live, but my Christ who lives in me, and the life I now live, I shall live by faith in the Son of God who loved me and, yes, gave His life for me. The Son of God, my Savior, truly lives!

JUDAS

An Easter Drama — Biblical Setting

The drama gives listeners an opportunity to see behind the character of Judas and to identify with their own struggles and inability to see the Christ for who He really was.

Setting: The night Judas received the thirty pieces of silver from the high priests to betray Jesus

Props: A bag full of coins; something to lean against — rock, sack, wall

Character:
JUDAS: A very intense and agonized individual who talks rapidly as though in great turmoil

Costume: Biblical dress; nothing on head so audience can see character's face

(Judas enters from a side aisle. His steps are rapid, his breathing hard. He continually looks around as though someone is following him. He clutches a money bag closely.)

JUDAS: *(Agitated)* Why is it that I always feel eyes peering at my back as though someone would rob me? *(Glances about)* The streets are deserted. Everyone's long gone to bed. There's nothing to fear. No one even knows I am about. *(Stops and looks nervously around, then fumblingly opens the bag and fingers the money)*
  (Relieved) It's all here, all thirty pieces of silver, just as they promised. I should have asked for more. Those whitewashed tombs

who call themselves priests of God didn't even bat an eye at my offer, so glad were they to avenge their hate. It was obvious they certainly didn't care about me ... pushed the money into my hands as if it were tainted and shoved me out the door, the back door, as if I were a beggar and a thief — *(sneeringly)* those miserable cowards cloaked with their feelings of pride and visions of greatness. The God of Abraham must look down from heaven and cringe at the sight. Phonies, all of them!

(Pauses, looks for a place in the shadows to hide and rest. Slumps down)

Judas, Judas, how did you get yourself in such a mess? For two long years, you've been a disciple of Jesus Christ, a man who claims to be the long-awaited Messiah, the one who will restore the kingdom to Israel. *(Sighs)*

Only God Himself knows how sick I am of Romans ... night and day breathing down on us like a lion after its prey. Money? Who has money? *(Disdainfully)* Only the mighty Romans and those hypocritical priests have money. The rest of us live like paupers. And I did — until Jesus put me in charge of the money bags. It was almost too easy.

Day after wretched day I watched Him heal the sick for no pay until the rest of us were so weary we could hardly hold up our heads. He could have made us all rich with His miracle powers. Unfortunately, He cared nothing for riches. It was as though compassion and love literally overwhelmed Him. *(Pause)* Amazing man, that Jesus.

(Wearily) For two years I have followed this prophet who claims to be the Son of God. *(Pause)* Seems rather foolish, but what else did I have to do? Even when He said, "I am the bread of life; he who eats my flesh and drinks my blood has eternal life," and many left Him, I still followed. His words were so full of life and hope ... I'll admit, I was drawn to Him. *(Disdainfully)* Peter, what a gullible fool, he swallowed it all. Claimed he'd even die with Him if need be. The rest of the disciples were the same. All except me. I sell out to no one! I, Judas Iscariot, am my own man.

(Sits up with conviction) Well, the time has come. I have my own agenda, my own life. If Jesus Christ is the Messiah, I say it's

time to prove it. Enough of ministering to the miserable wretches of this world. What worth are they? Day after endless day they hound us. If Jesus is who He says He is, it's time for Him to get on with establishing a kingdom. If He is the Christ, let Him call His angels when things get tough. And if He's only a man, well, I guess it's just as well the world finds out now. Either way, I have my money.

(Opens sack and runs fingers through money) Judas, money is all you've ever wanted. Look what you hold in your hands. Money gets you everything! You can now know a depth of happiness that you've never experienced before in your life. You have power, prestige ... *(Pause)* So why do you feel so empty ... what is this overpowering yearning to sit next to the Master? Has He had so great a hold on you? *(Quietly)* To feel His gentle gaze upon my cheeks ... to see His boundless love for me even when He knew I was daily robbing from His funds ...

(Jumps up) Judas! You have gone mad! Forget the love! Forget the compassion! It's time this man, Jesus of Nazareth, be revealed for who He really is. Yes. I, Judas Iscariot, will betray Him. *(Hurries off into the night)*

HE IS RISEN

A Biblical-day Play

This play is especially written for Easter Sunday. It is designed to be used in the Sunday morning worship service.

Setting: A quiet, secluded place

Props: Draped box or chair for Mary

Characters:
1ST WOMAN: Young, vibrant Christian woman
2ND WOMAN: Young, vibrant Christian woman
3RD WOMAN: An older Christian woman
MARY: An older woman with much grace and inner strength

Time: Easter Sunday

Costumes: Biblical dress

(Mary is sitting quietly on stage center left, not moving, shoulders stooped, in deep thought, obviously disturbed. 1st, 2nd, 3rd women come up center aisle in excited conversation. They are half running, half walking, their hands moving about. Women rush up to Mary. They surround her with great excitement.)

1ST WOMAN: *(Shaking Mary's shoulder excitedly)* Mary, Mary, I have seen Him. I have seen the Christ. He is risen!

2ND WOMAN: *(Kneeling at Mary's feet. She interrupts)* It is true, Mary! Everything He said is true! Did He not say, "Destroy this temple and I will rebuild it in three days?"

3RD WOMAN: *(Taking Mary's face in her hands)* We have seen Him, Mary. We have seen the Christ. We knelt at His feet, His wonderful feet. And His eyes, Mary. Oh, His eyes ... they were so full of compassion, so understanding, so filled with love our hearts could hardly contain it. It was as though we had been washed, as though His very gaze made us completely new.

1ST WOMAN: Mary, we know how hard it is for you to believe — even we can hardly believe it ourselves. His death on the cross, His agony, His suffering. But the tomb is empty! The stone has been rolled from the door! We saw it! All three of us. Mary, your son, the Christ, is no longer dead!

2ND WOMAN: The guards told us there was a great earthquake and a bright light.

1ST WOMAN: We thought they were lying, but when we looked inside the tomb ...

2ND WOMAN: There were angels, Mary, two of them. And they shone like a million suns ... our eyes could not even look upon their faces. And they said to us, "Why seek ye the living among the dead?"

1ST WOMAN: They told us not to be afraid, that Jesus was not there, that He had risen as He said. And we are to take word to the brethren to leave for Galilee, and there we will see Him.

3RD WOMAN: Mary, we are on our way now to tell Peter. Come ... come with us. He is risen, the Christ is risen.

MARY: *(Shakes her head, talks slowly as in a daze)* No, leave me, my sisters. Your words bring no understanding to my heart. They are too much for me. Let me sit here for a few minutes. My mind must have time to think ...

(Each woman hugs Mary in turn. They excitedly take their leave, still chatting. Mary sits with her face toward heaven, in deep agony. For a long time she remains silent. When she finally speaks, her thoughts are slow.)

MARY: He is risen ... the Christ is risen ... Why cannot my heart comprehend those words? *(Pause)* No, He was never an ordinary man. There were so many things about Him that were so puzzling ... I knew when the prophet Simon told me in the temple that a sword would pierce my very soul, to the end that thoughts from many hearts would be revealed, that I had become part of a plan I understood nothing about. A walk of faith that would bring me no friends ... no glory ... A walk God chose for me only because I believed in Him. *(Pause)*

And there were so many times I didn't understand. Who can understand your own son, God's Son, raising people from the grave ... His great love, His determination to die for the sins of the world ... a world that didn't deserve Him. Yes, the Mighty One has done great things for me and holy is His name.

(Rises, becomes more excited) They say He is risen ... risen ... risen ... That He is alive, just as He said. They say they have seen Him ... heard Him ... touched Him ... *(Pauses)* And in my heart I know it is true. *(Mary becomes more confident, more radiant)* Don't ask me how I know, I just suddenly know. The Christ is risen! Death has been swallowed up in victory. Oh, I see it now! It is a new day! A new era!

Yes, I will go to Galilee. I will see my son, my Lord, the Savior of the world. Yes, the Christ is risen! The plan of God is at last complete. I ... will see ... the Christ!

(Mary hurries off down the center aisle)